WITHDRAWN

How I Care
for My Pet

by Jennifer Boothroyd

Lerner Publications Company · Minneapolis

LERNER

SOURCE

Expand learning beyond the printed book. Download free, complementary educational resources for this book from our website, www.lerneresource.com.

The images in this book are used with the permission of: © Todd Strand/Independent Picture Service.

Front Cover: © Todd Strand/Independent Picture Service.

Main body text set in ITC Avant Garde Gothic Std Medium 21/25.
Typeface provided by Adobe Systems.

Lerner Publications Company
A division of Lerner Publishing Group, Inc.
241 First Avenue North
Minneapolis, MN 55401 USA

For reading levels and more information, look up this title at www.lernerbooks.com.

Library of Congress Cataloging-in-Publication Data

Boothroyd, Jennifer, 1972–
    How I care for my pet / Jennifer Boothroyd.
        pages   cm. — (First step nonfiction – responsibility in action)
    Includes index.
    ISBN 978–1–4677–3632–9 (lib. bdg. : alk. paper)
    ISBN 978–1–4677–3645–9 (eBook)
    [1. Pets—Juvenile literature.] I. Title.
SF416.2.B67 2014
636.088'7—dc23   2013026970

Manufactured in the United States of America
1 – BP – 12/31/13

Table of Contents

My Dog Max

Max **depends** on me.

I need to take care of him.

Time to Eat

First, I fill his food dish.

Next, I fill his water dish.

Then Max eats and drinks.

Max needs to go outside.

I put on his **leash**.

I take him on a walk.

I clean up after him.

After Max's walk, we play in the yard.

We play **fetch**. First, I
throw the ball.

Then he runs to get it.
Finally, he brings it back.

Keeping Clean

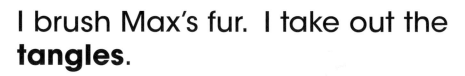

I brush Max's fur. I take out the **tangles**.

Tomorrow I will give him a bath.

That's how I care for my
pet.

How would you do it?

Activity

Write a Story

Pretend that you are responsible for taking care of a pet. On a separate sheet of paper, write a story about the steps that you would take to do this job. Use at least three of the words shown on the opposite page to write your story.

Story Word List

first

next

then

last

before

after

finally

Fun Facts

- The Labrador retriever is the most popular dog breed in the United States.

- Bella and Max are the most popular puppy names.

- There are more than 78 million pet dogs in the United States.

Glossary

depends – to need or count on for help

fetch – a game played with a dog where a human throws something and the dog brings it back

leash – a strap for holding an animal

tangles – knotted clumps of fur

Index